Animal Legs

By Connor Stratton

level
2
little blue
readers

www.littlebluehousebooks.com

Little Blue House is distributed by North Star Editions:
sales@northstareditions.com | 888-417-0195

Produced for Little Blue House by Red Line Editorial.

Photographs ©: iStockphoto, cover, 4, 6–7, 8–9, 10–11, 12, 15, 16–17, 18, 21 (top), 21 (bottom), 23 (top), 23 (bottom), 24 (top left), 24 (top right), 24 (bottom left), 24 (bottom right)

Library of Congress Control Number: 2020900792

ISBN
978-1-64619-177-2 (hardcover)
978-1-64619-211-3 (paperback)
978-1-64619-279-3 (ebook pdf)
978-1-64619-245-8 (hosted ebook)

Printed in the United States of America
Mankato, MN
082020

About the Author

Connor Stratton enjoys spotting new animals and writing books for children. He lives in Minnesota.

Table of Contents

leg

Run, Swim, Hop

Many animals have legs.
Animals use their legs in
different ways.

Some animals run with their legs.

Some animals swim with their legs.

Some animals hop with their legs.

So Many Legs

Many animals have

two legs.

Ostriches have two legs.

Many animals have four legs.

Giraffes have four legs.

Giraffes have the longest legs on Earth.

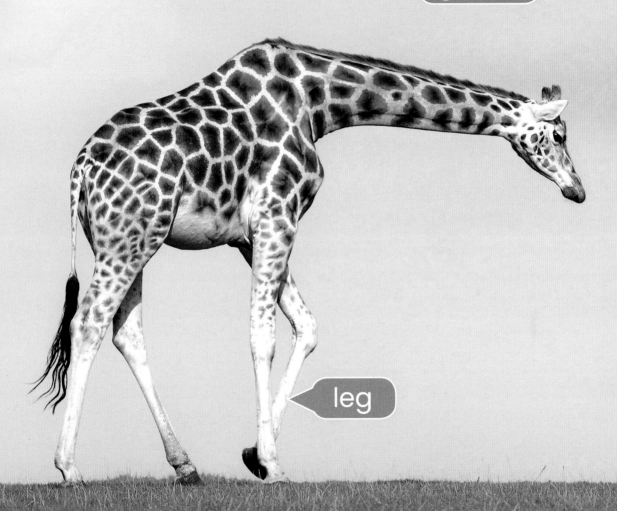

giraffe

leg

Animals can have more than four legs. Millipedes have hundreds of legs.

Feet

Many animals have feet.

Feet are the lowest parts of legs.

Some feet are paws.

Some feet are hooves.

Horses have hooves.

Some feet have claws.

Birds can have claws.

Glossary

bird

horse

giraffe

ostrich

Index